MY SICKO BOSS

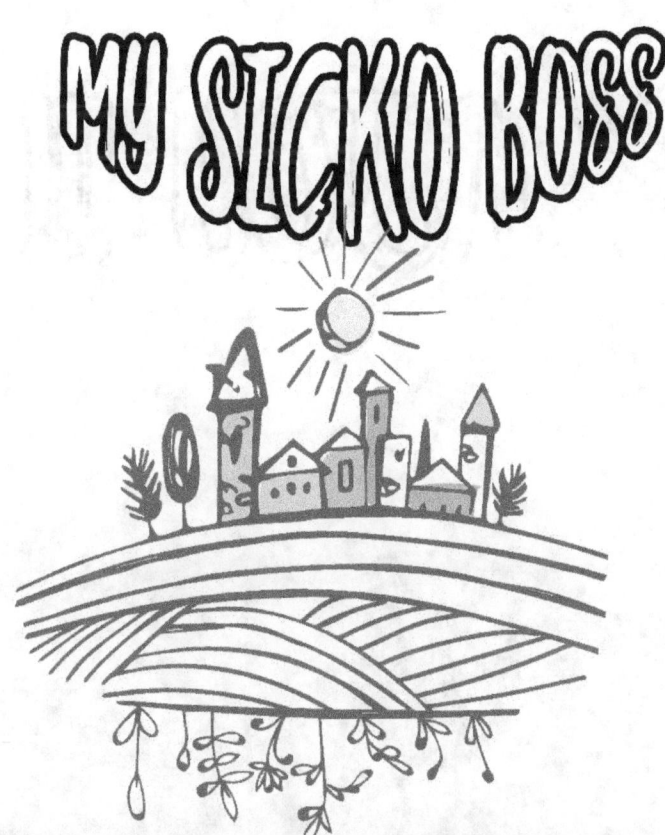

Funny Swear Worlds Coloring Book for Release Stress

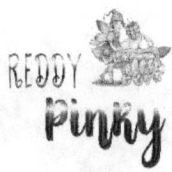

REDDY
Pinky

ENJOY !!!

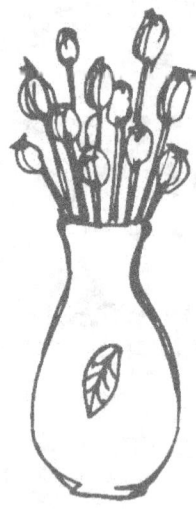

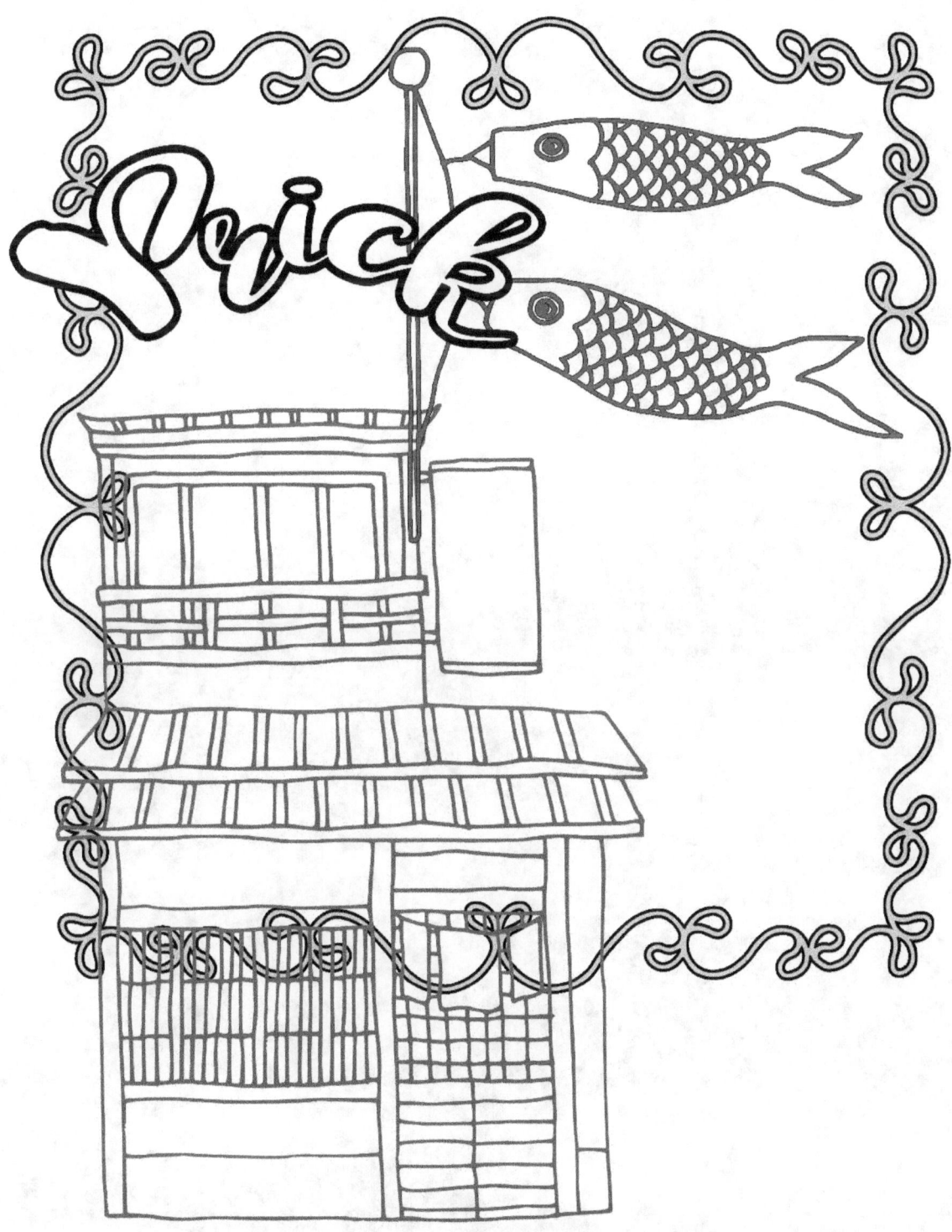

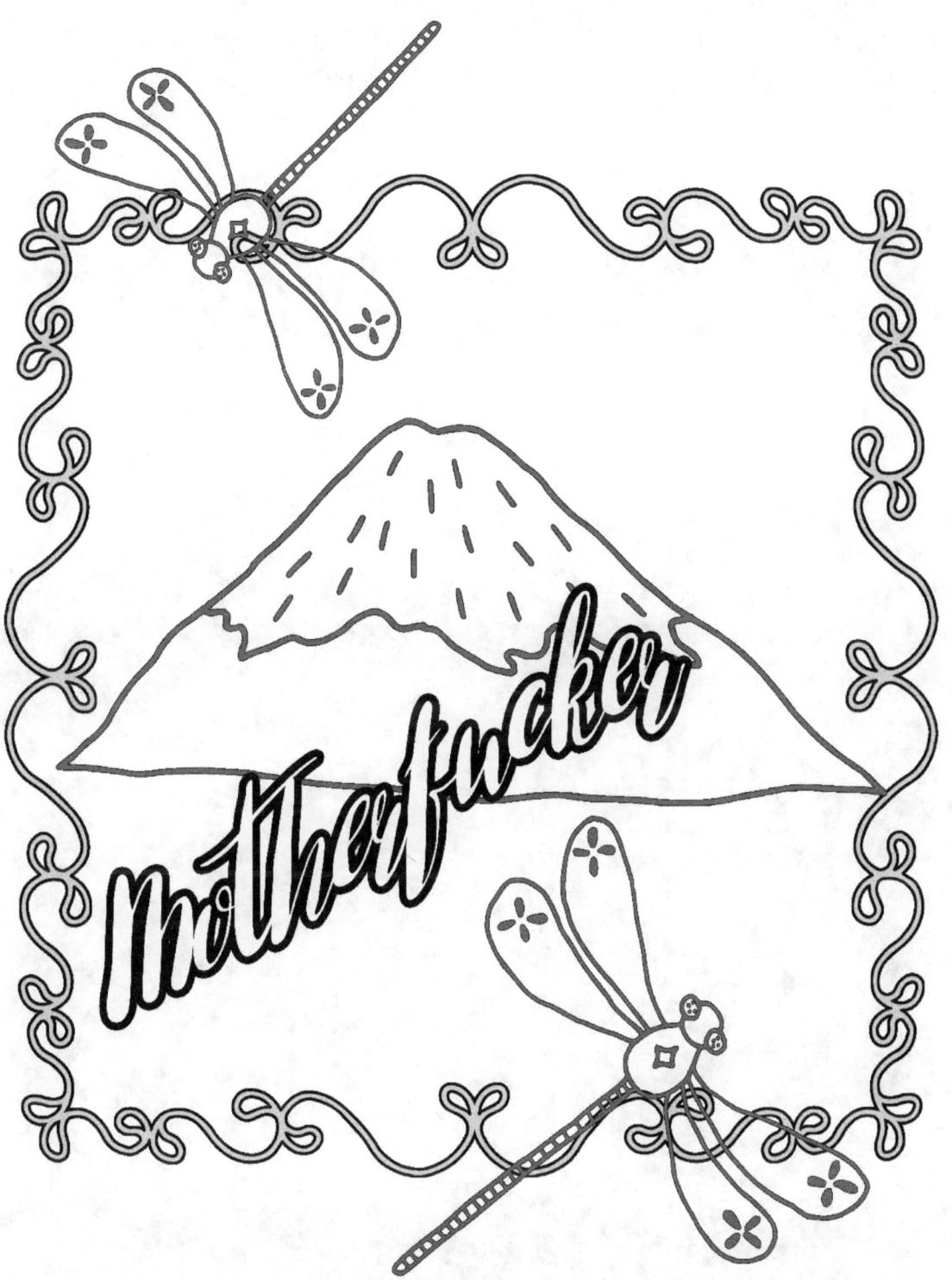

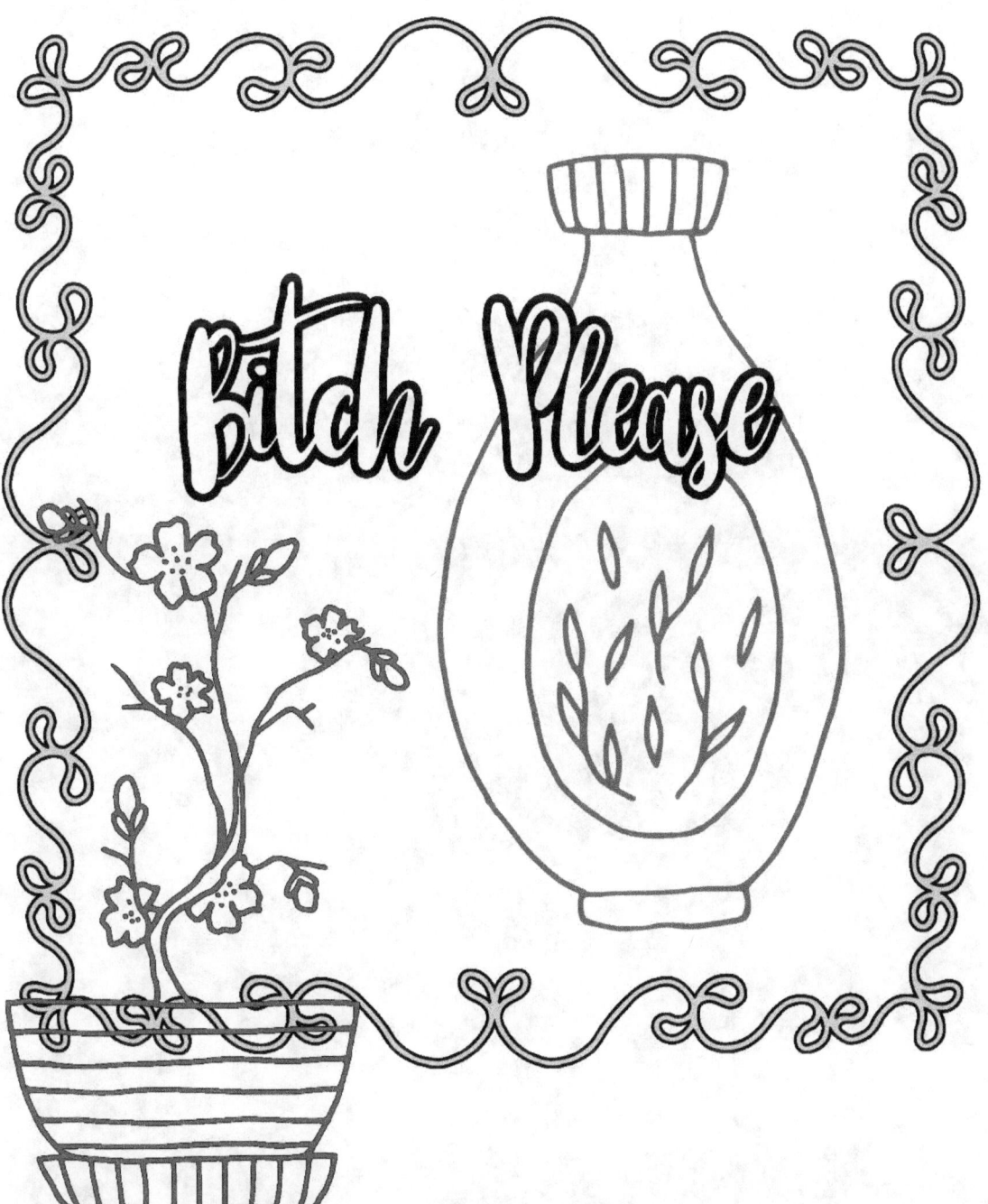

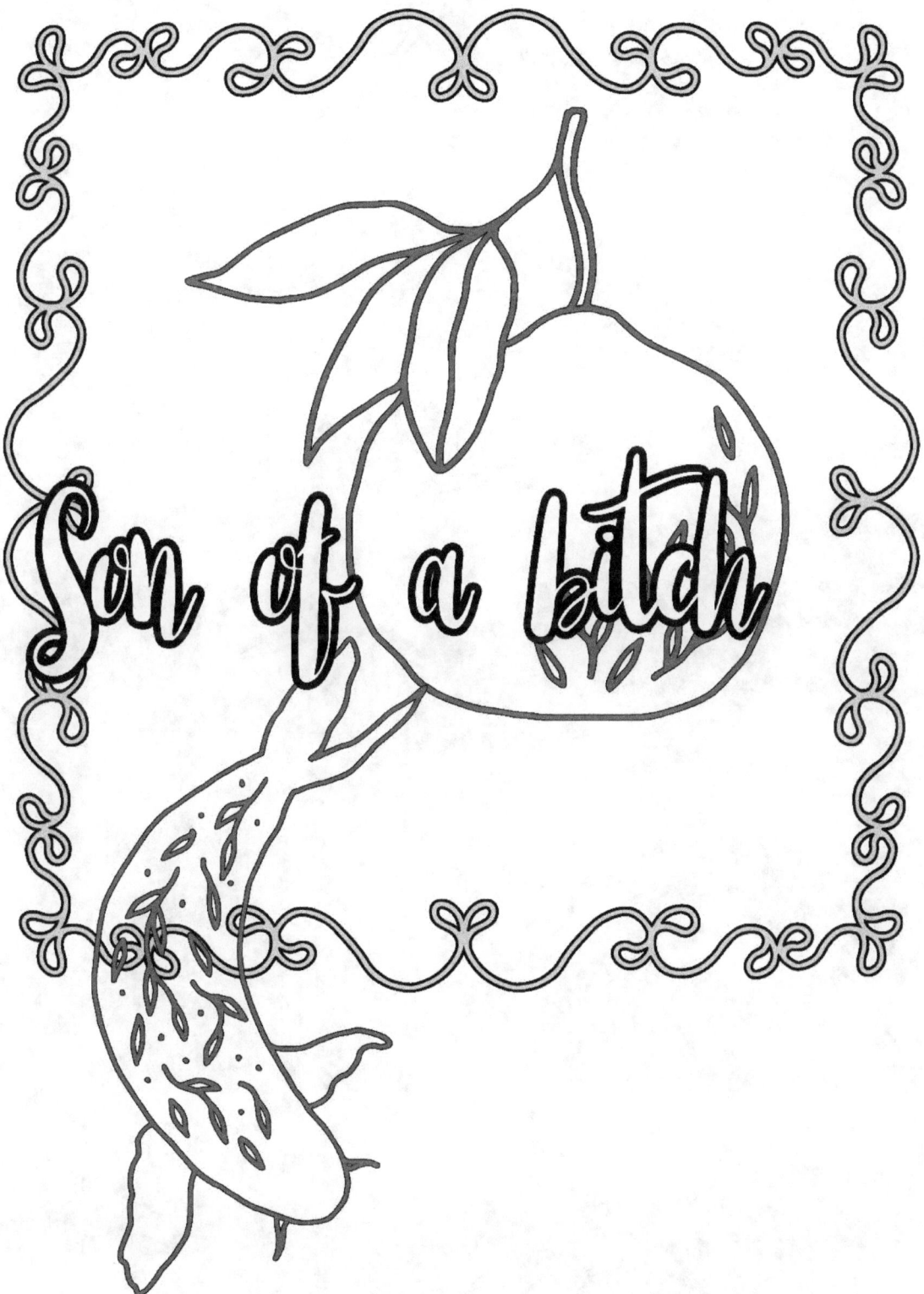

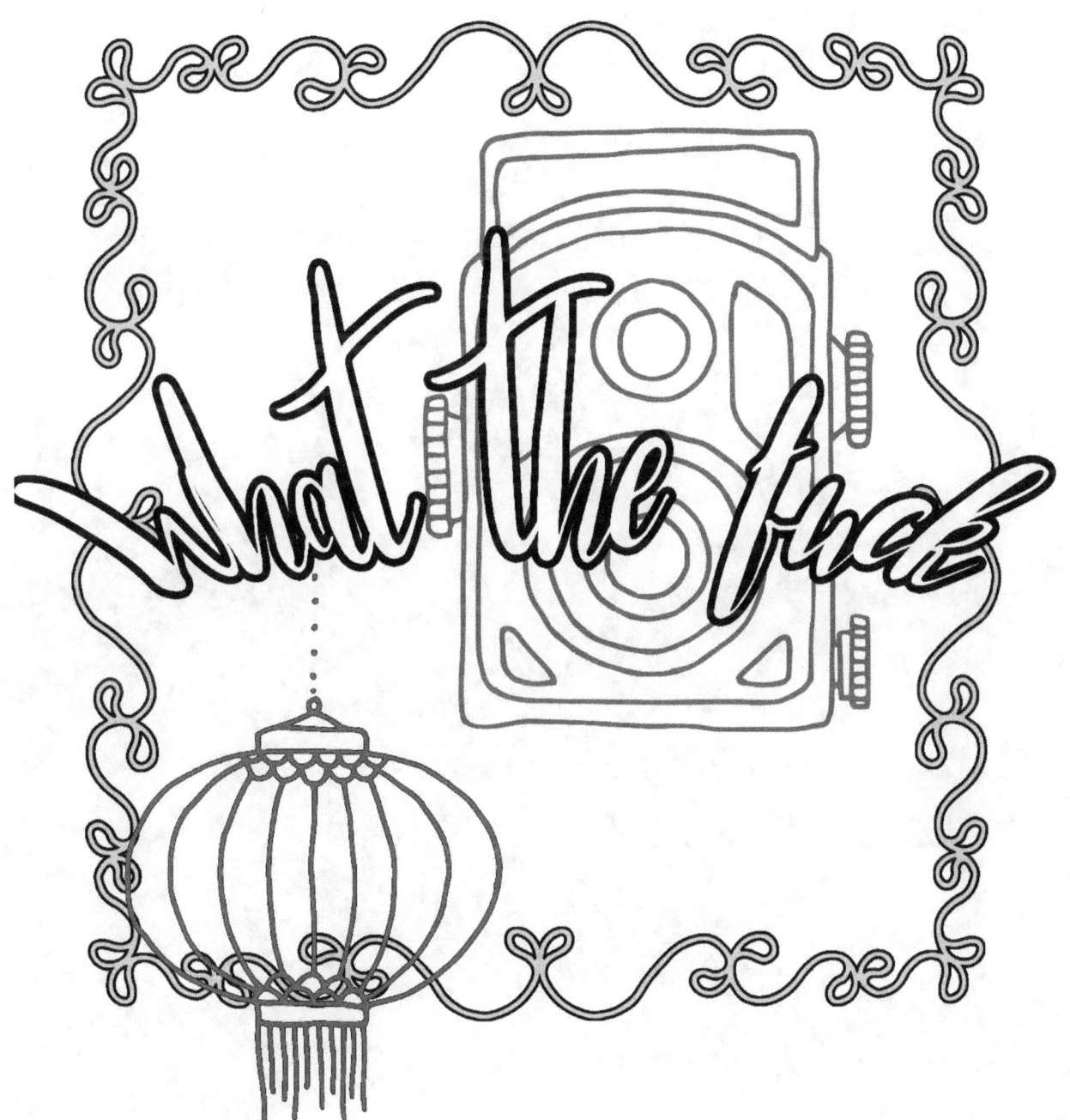

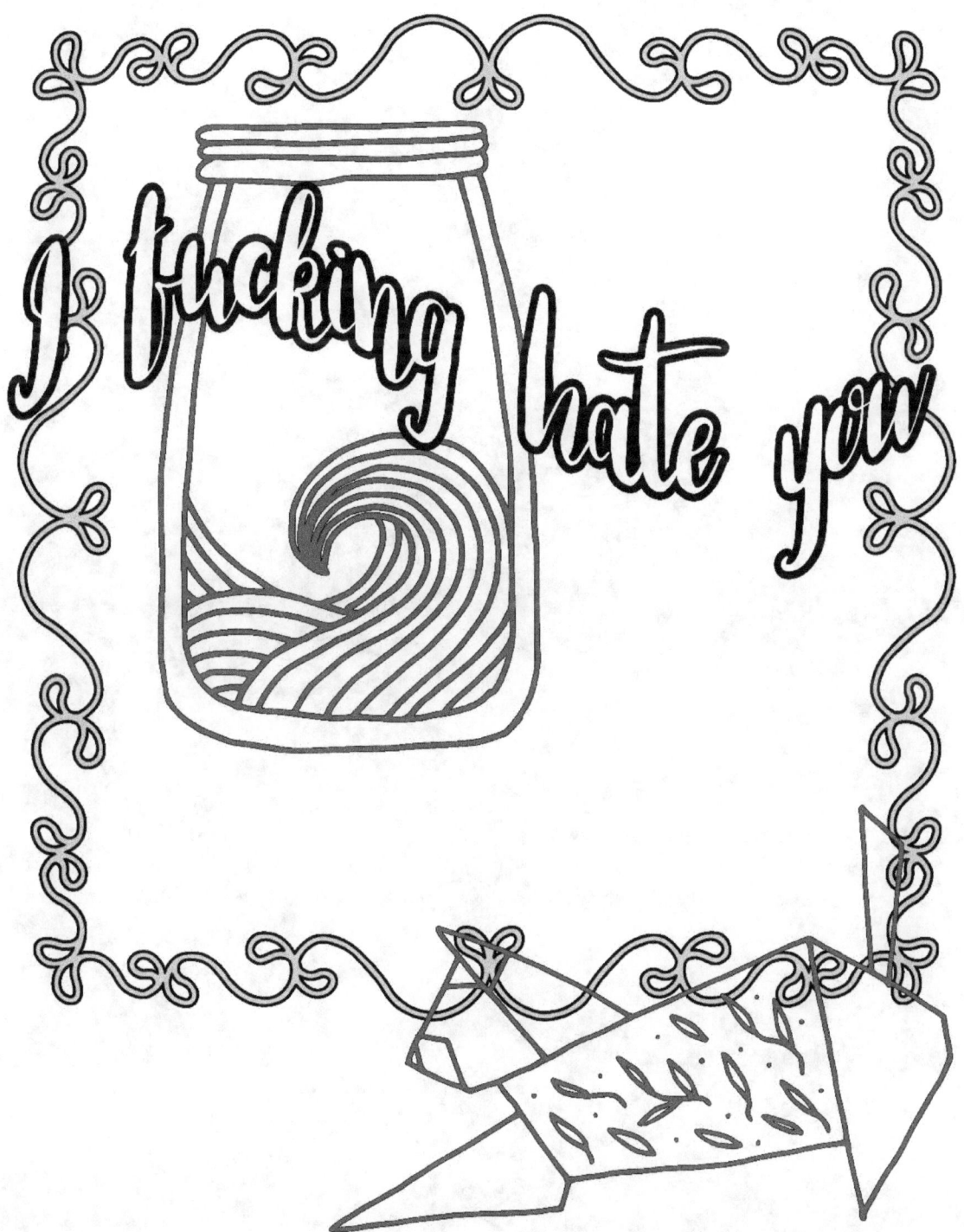

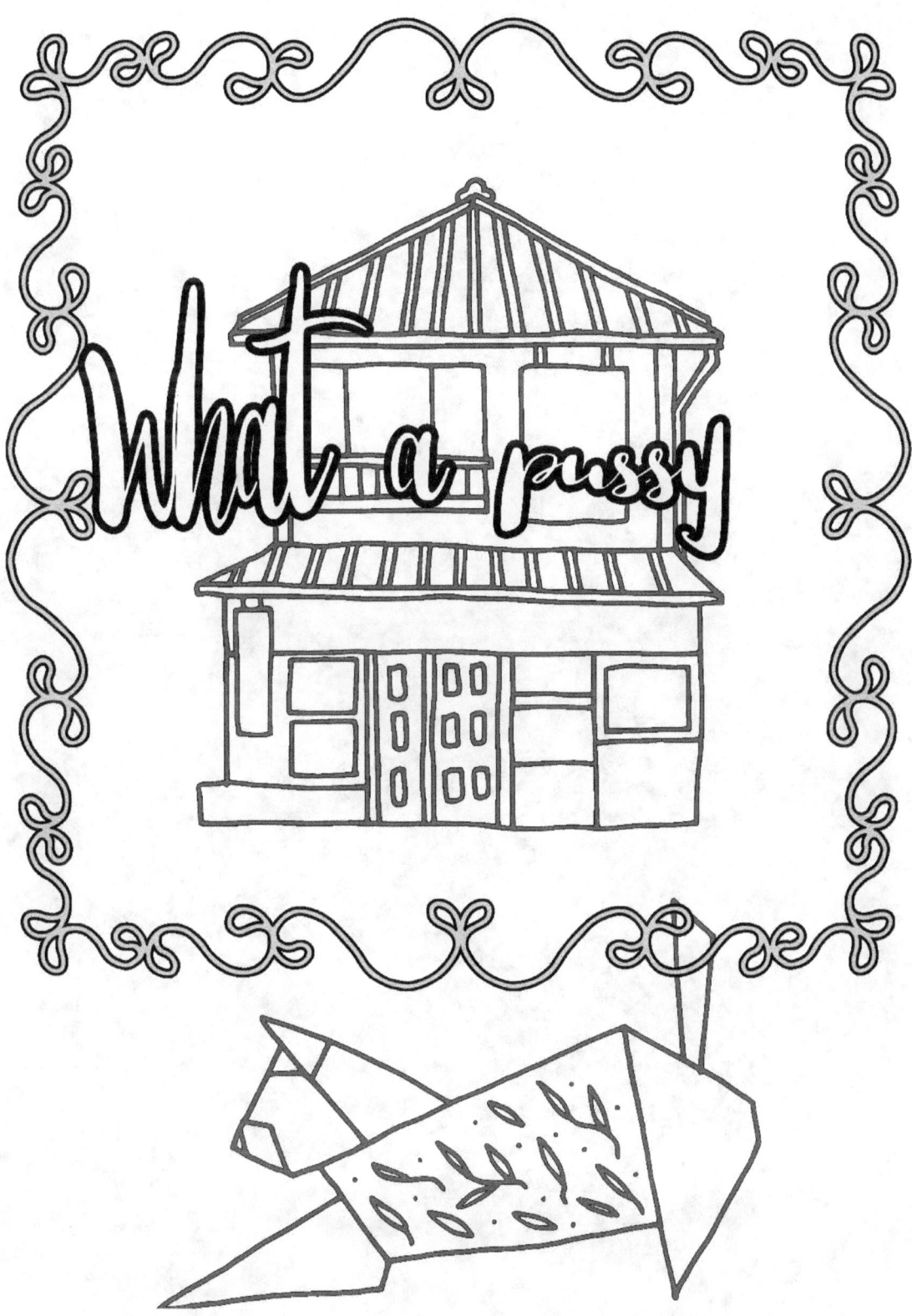

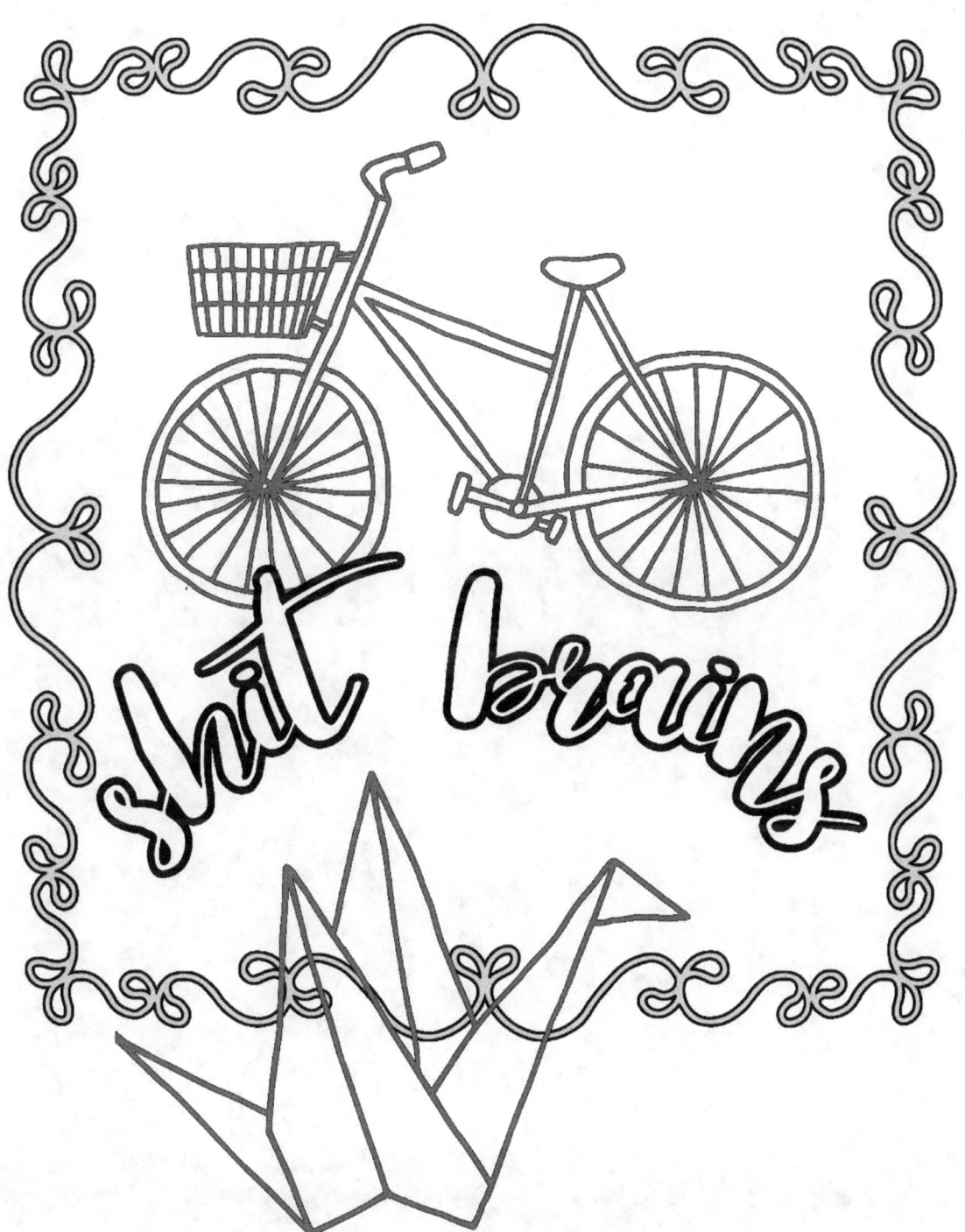

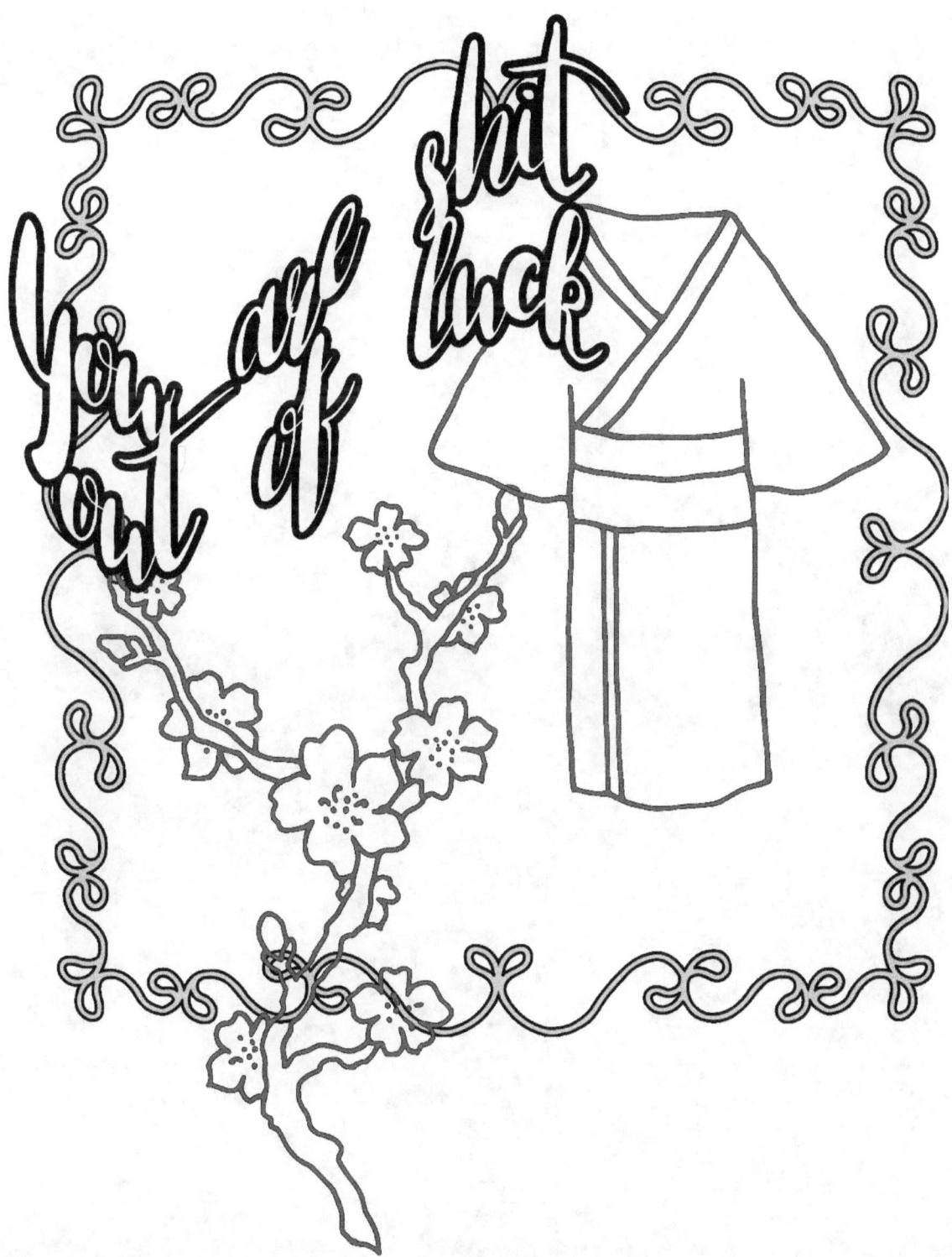

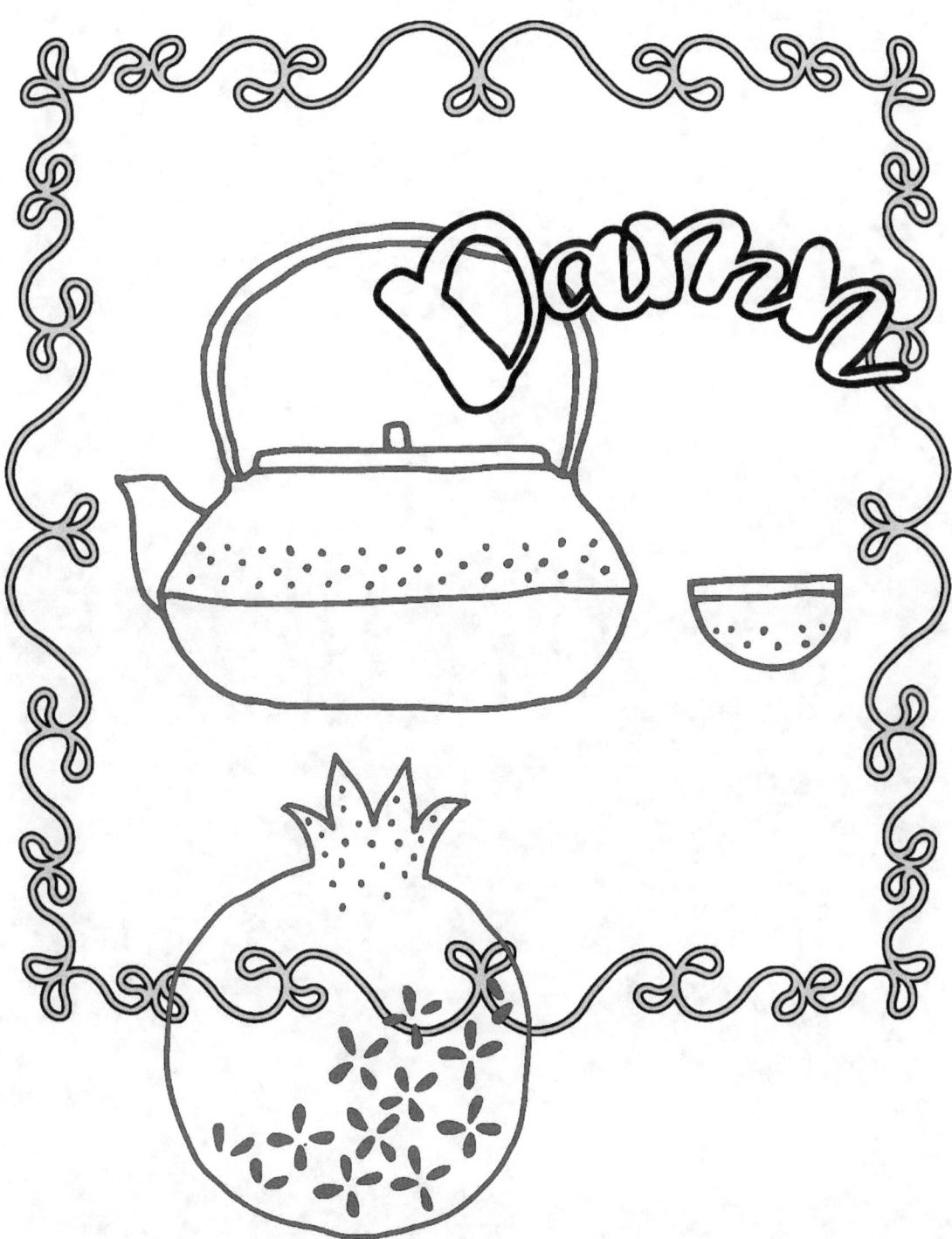

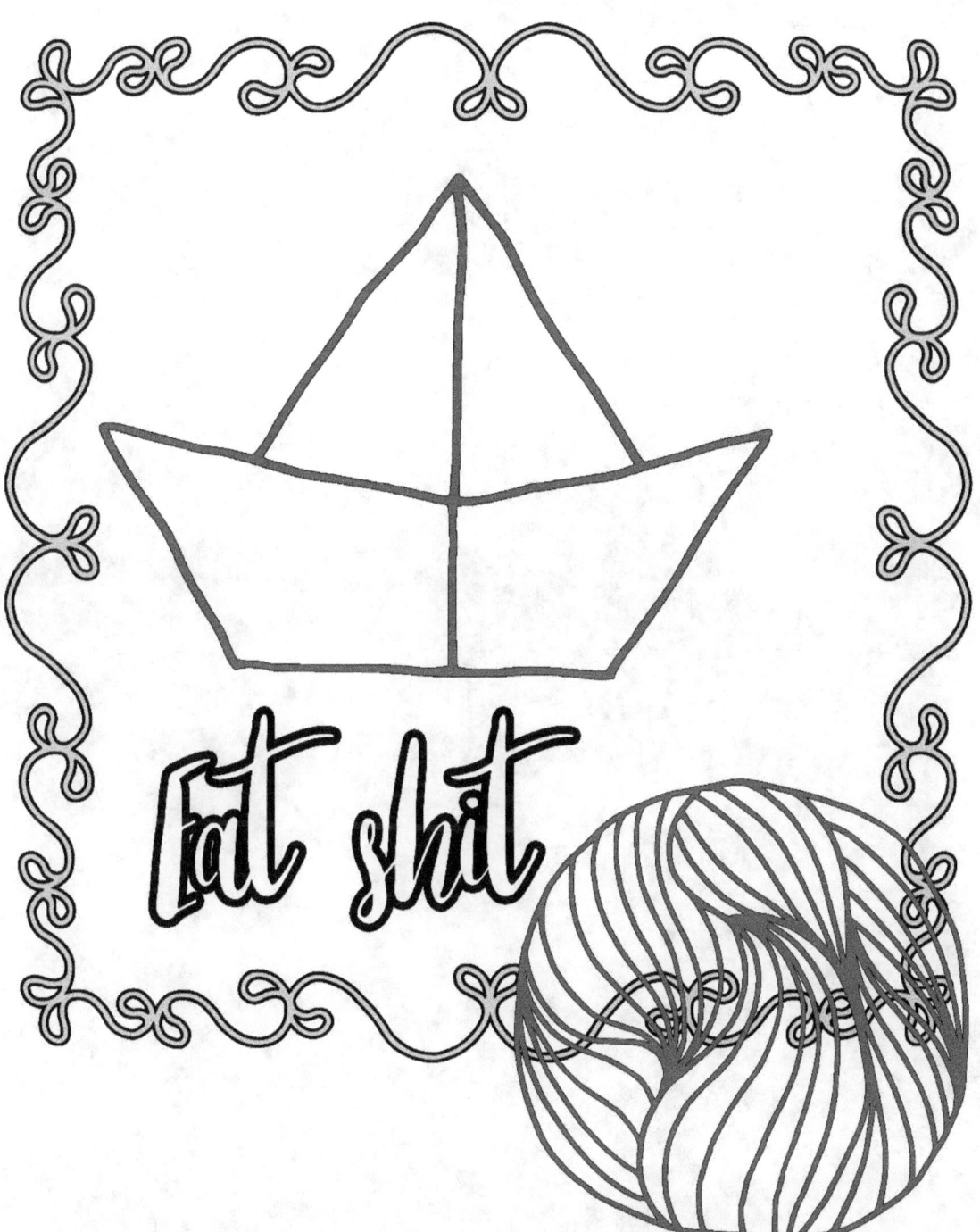

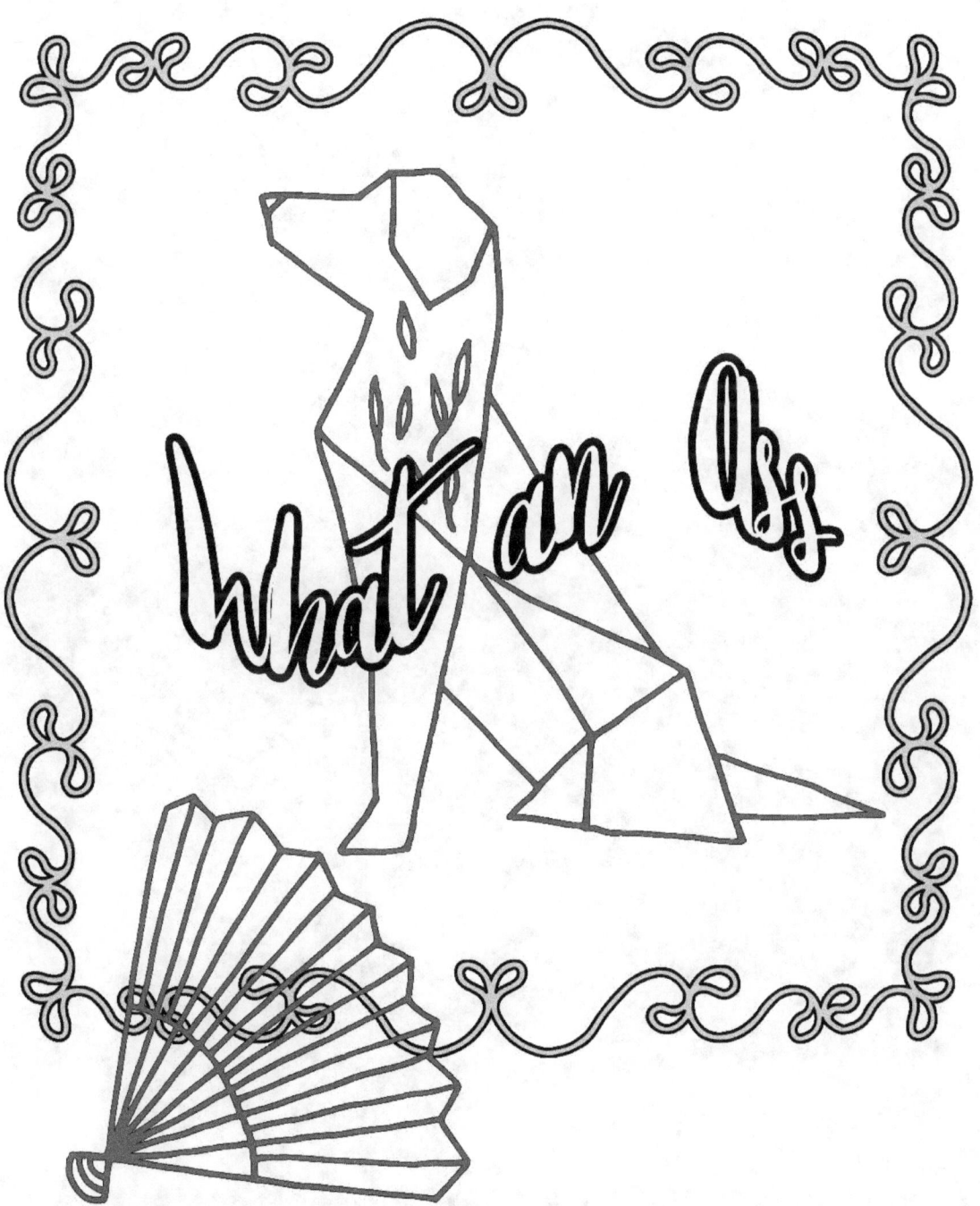

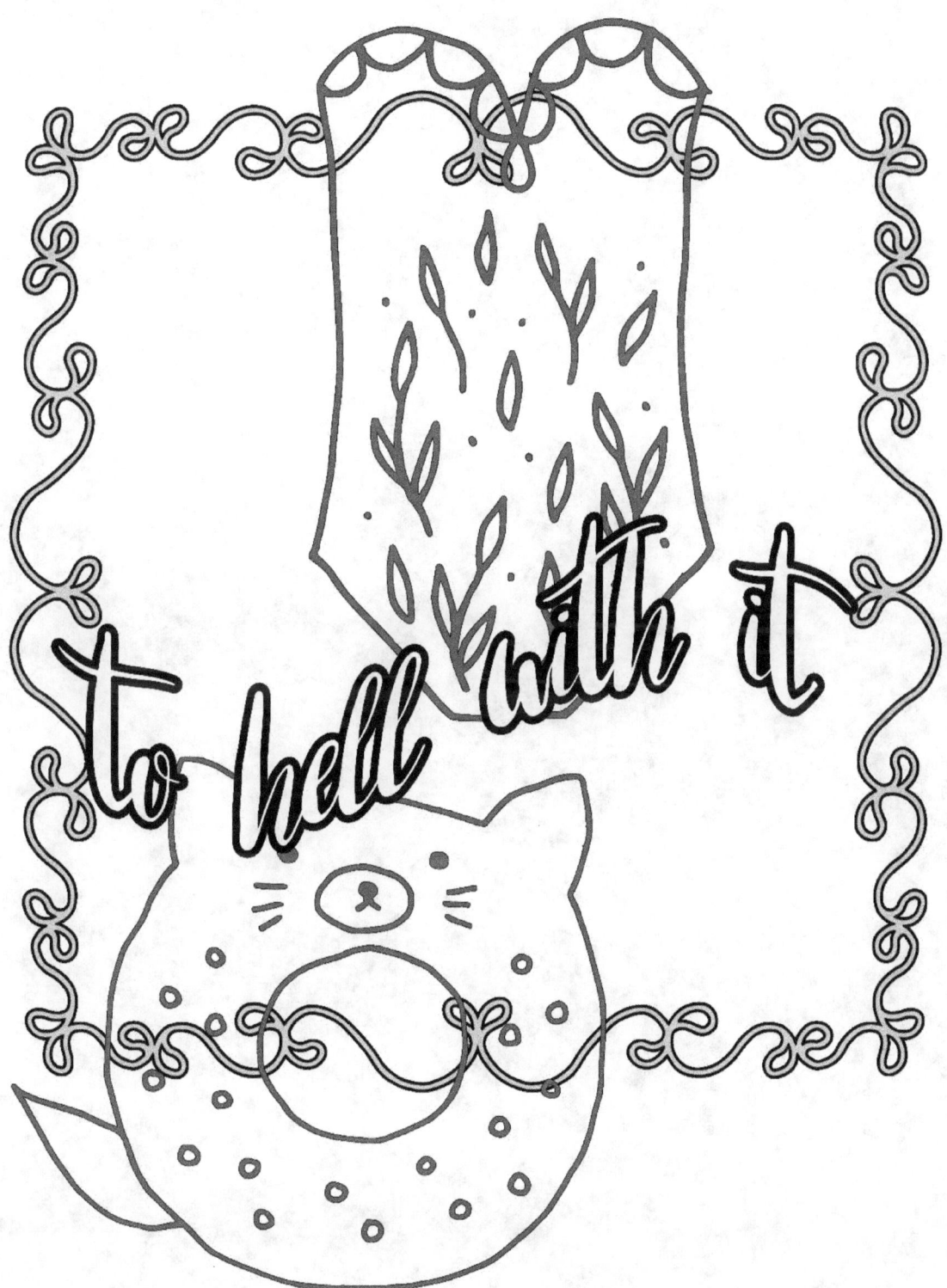

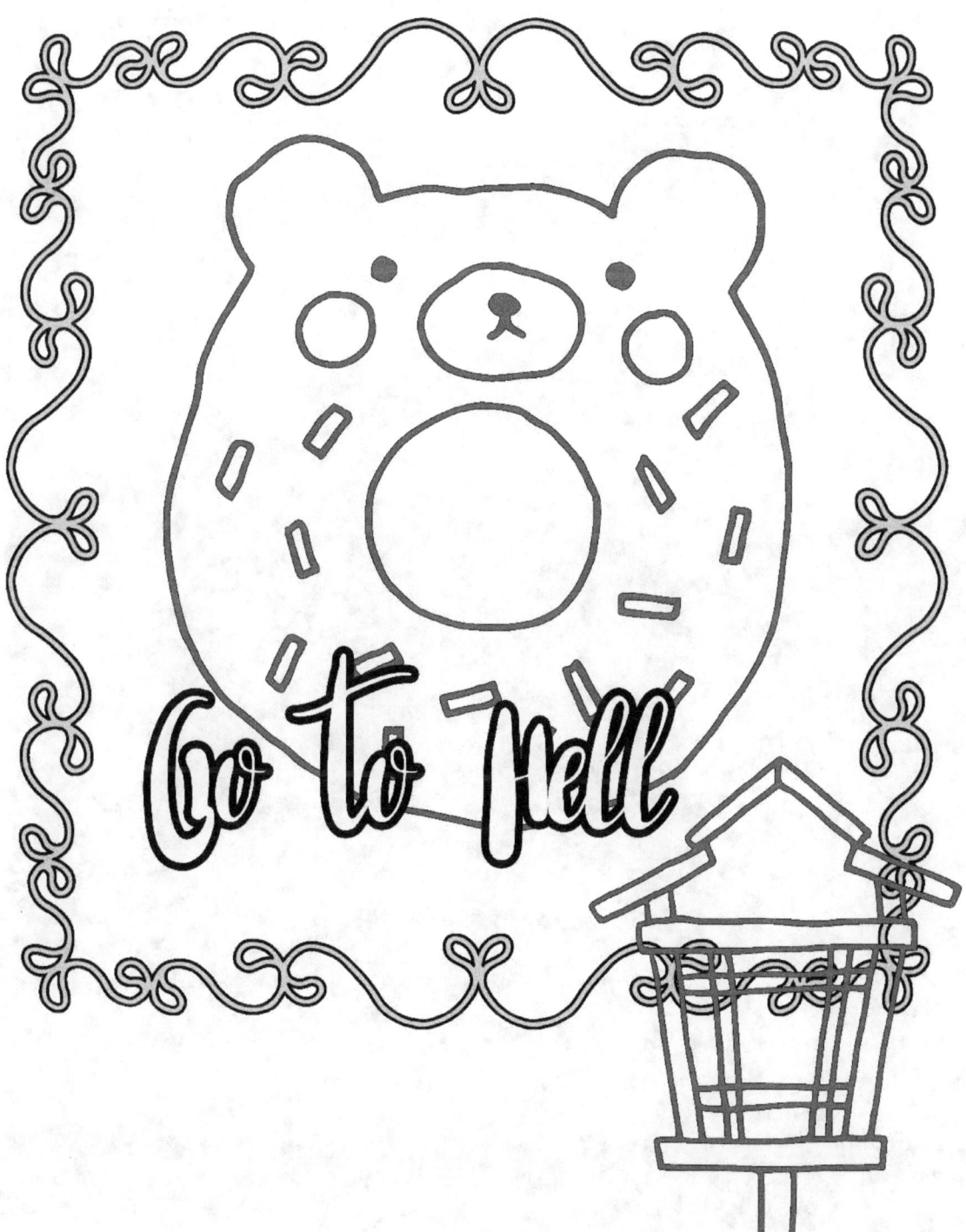

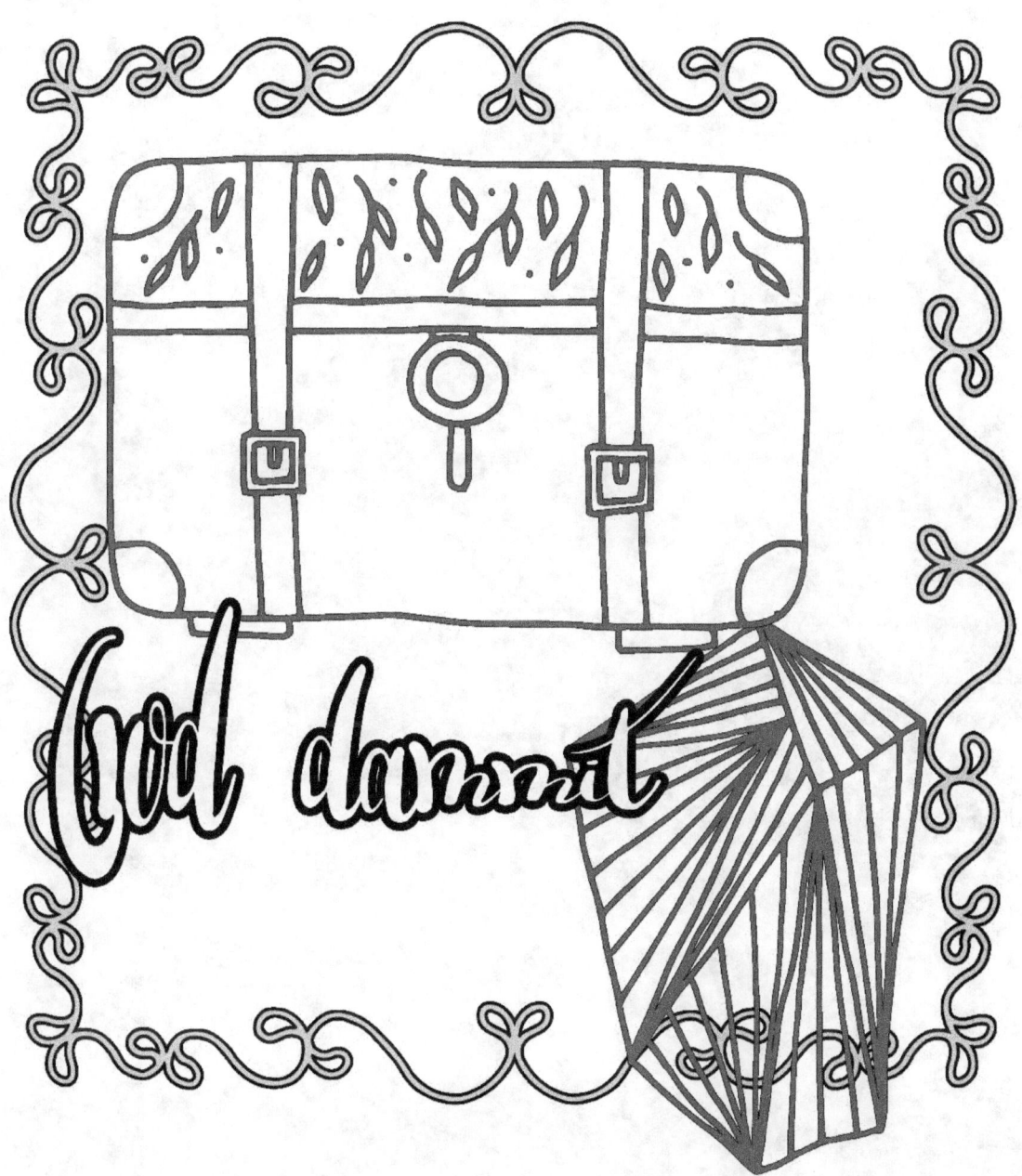

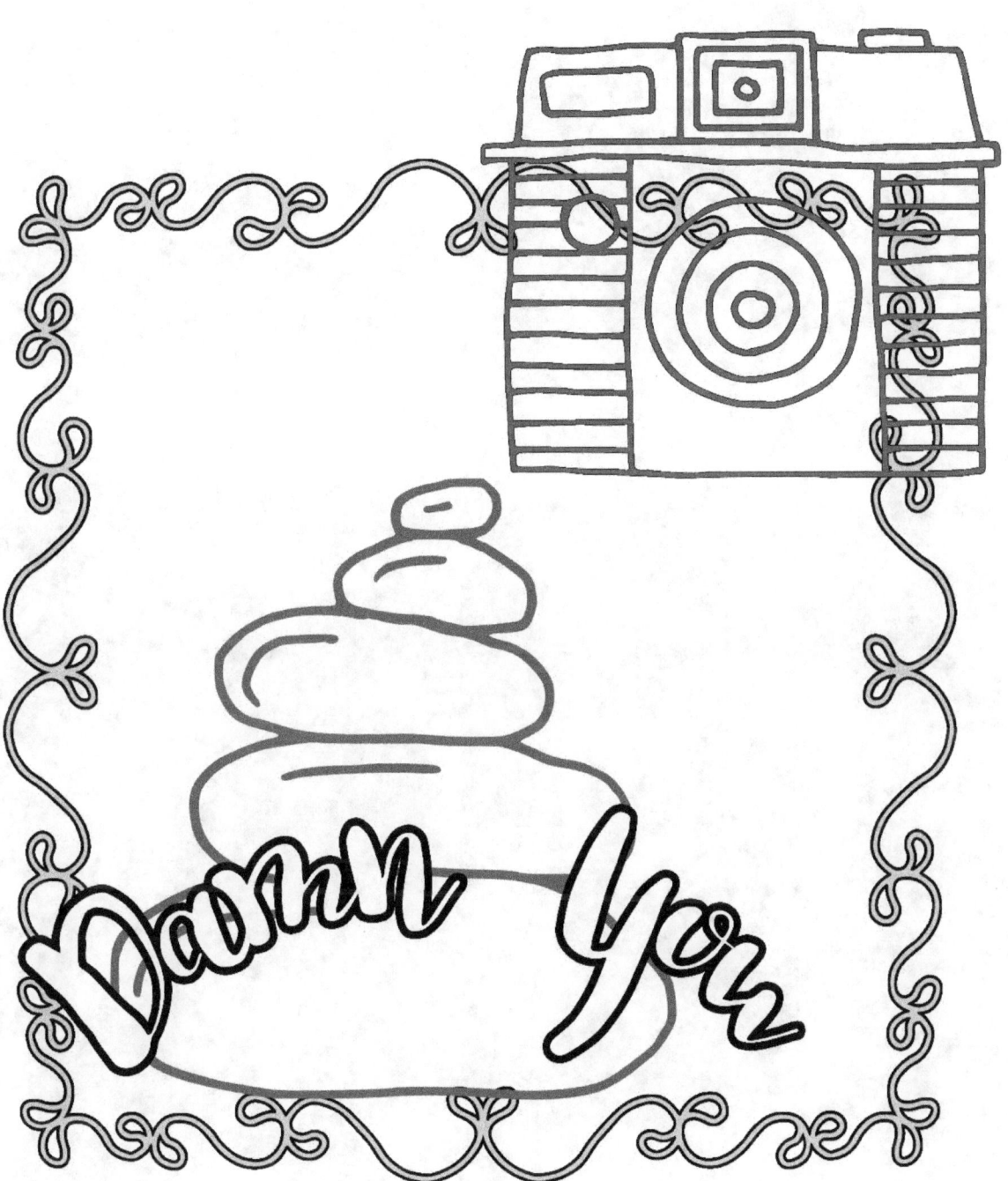

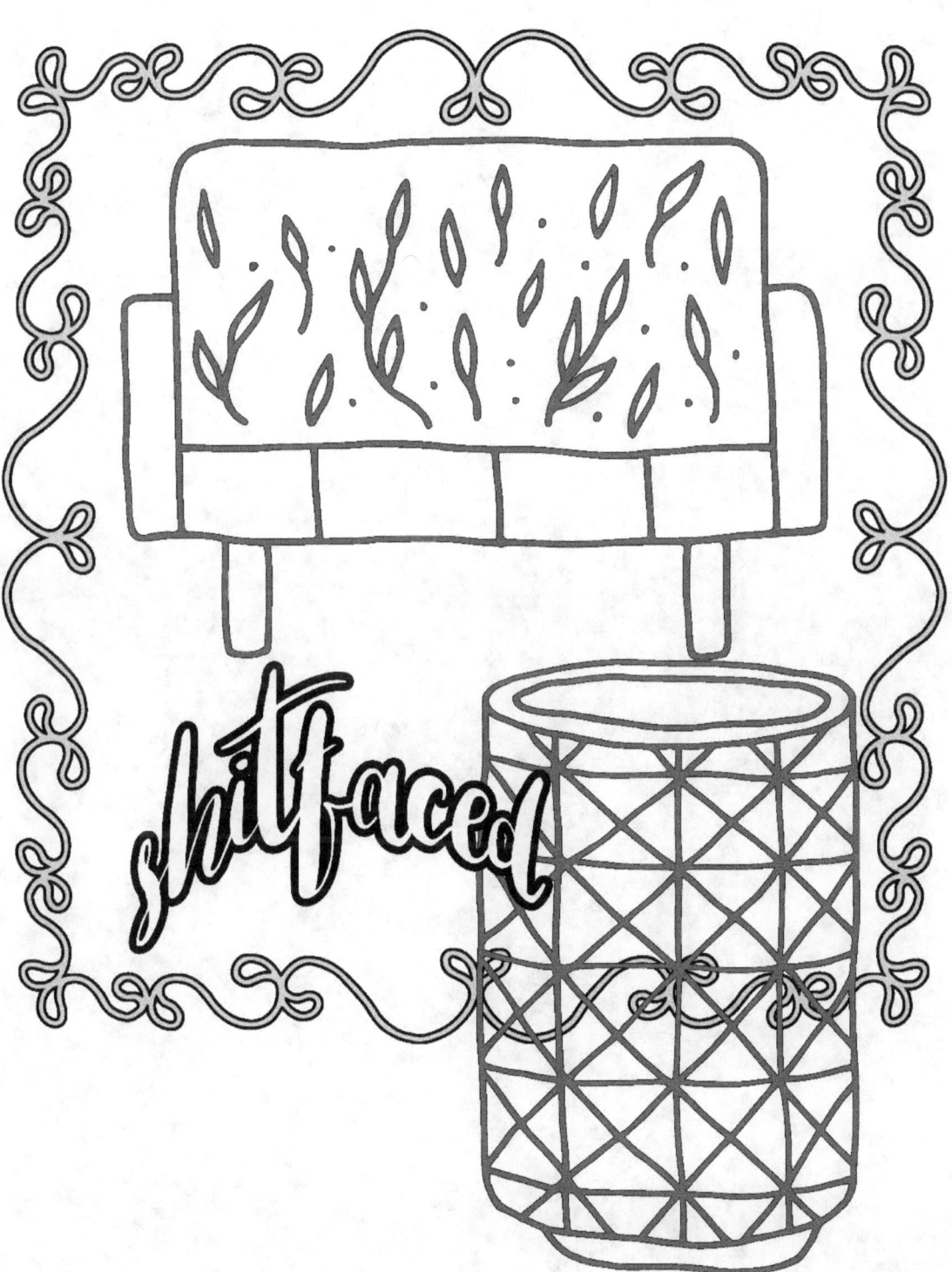

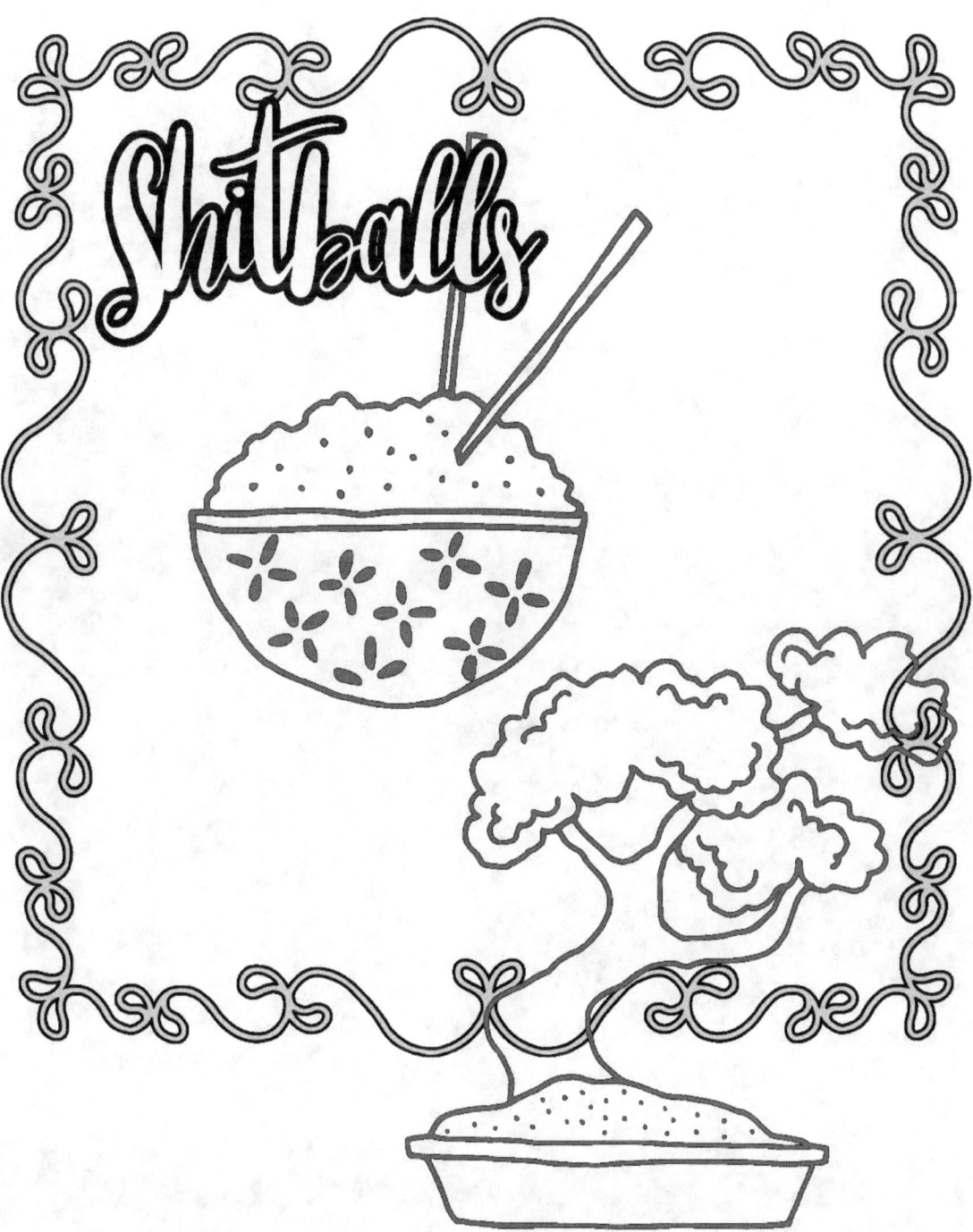

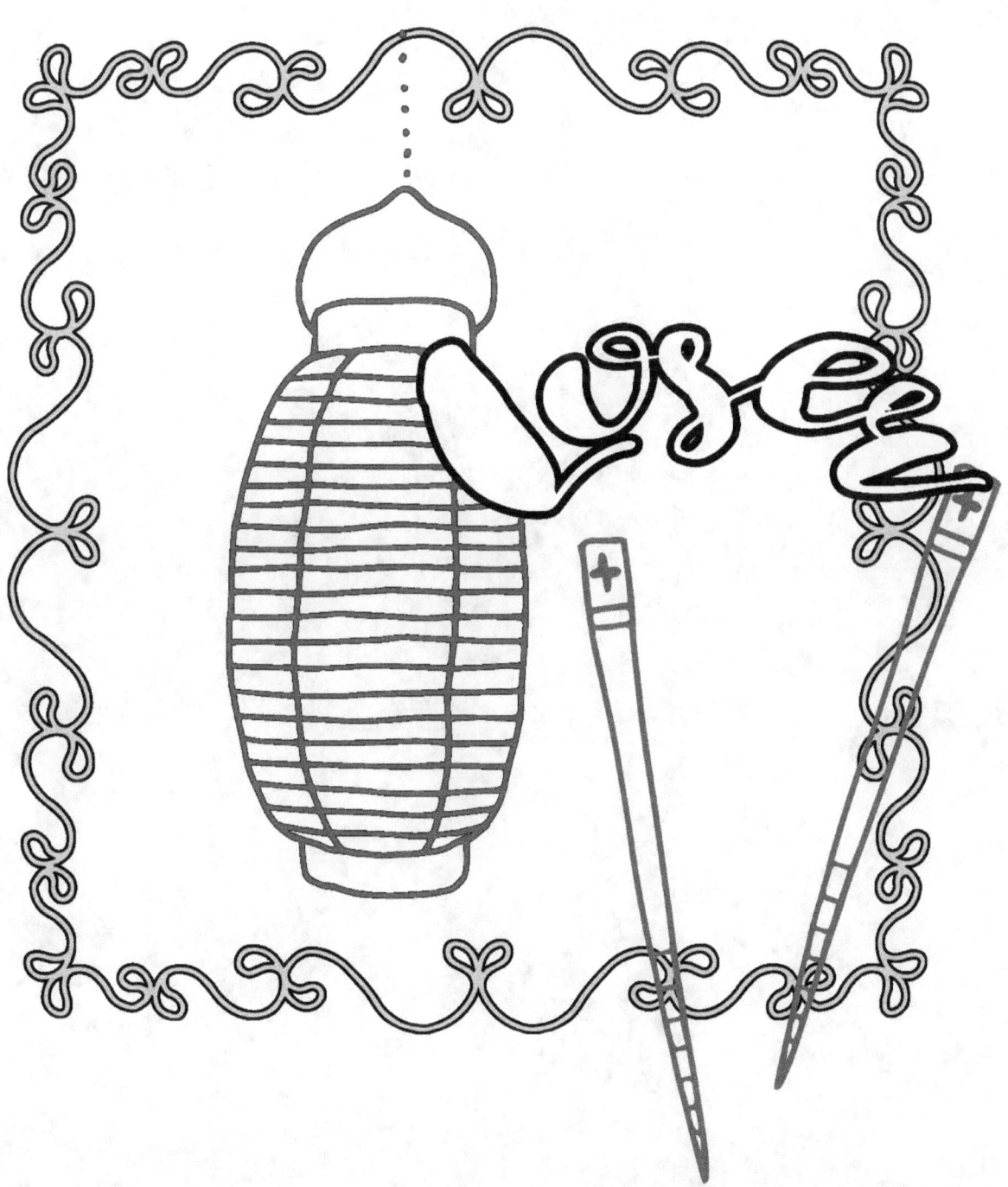

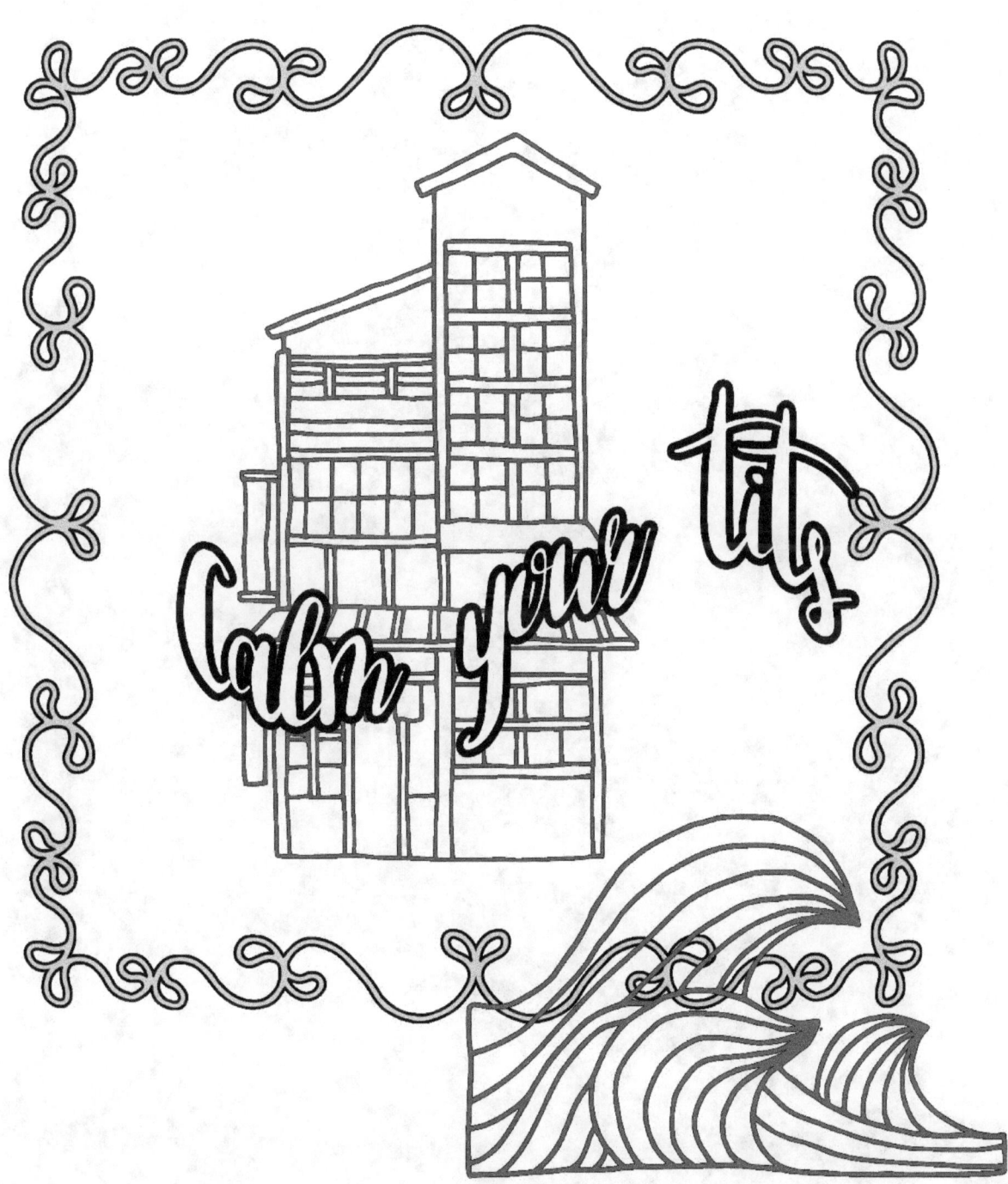

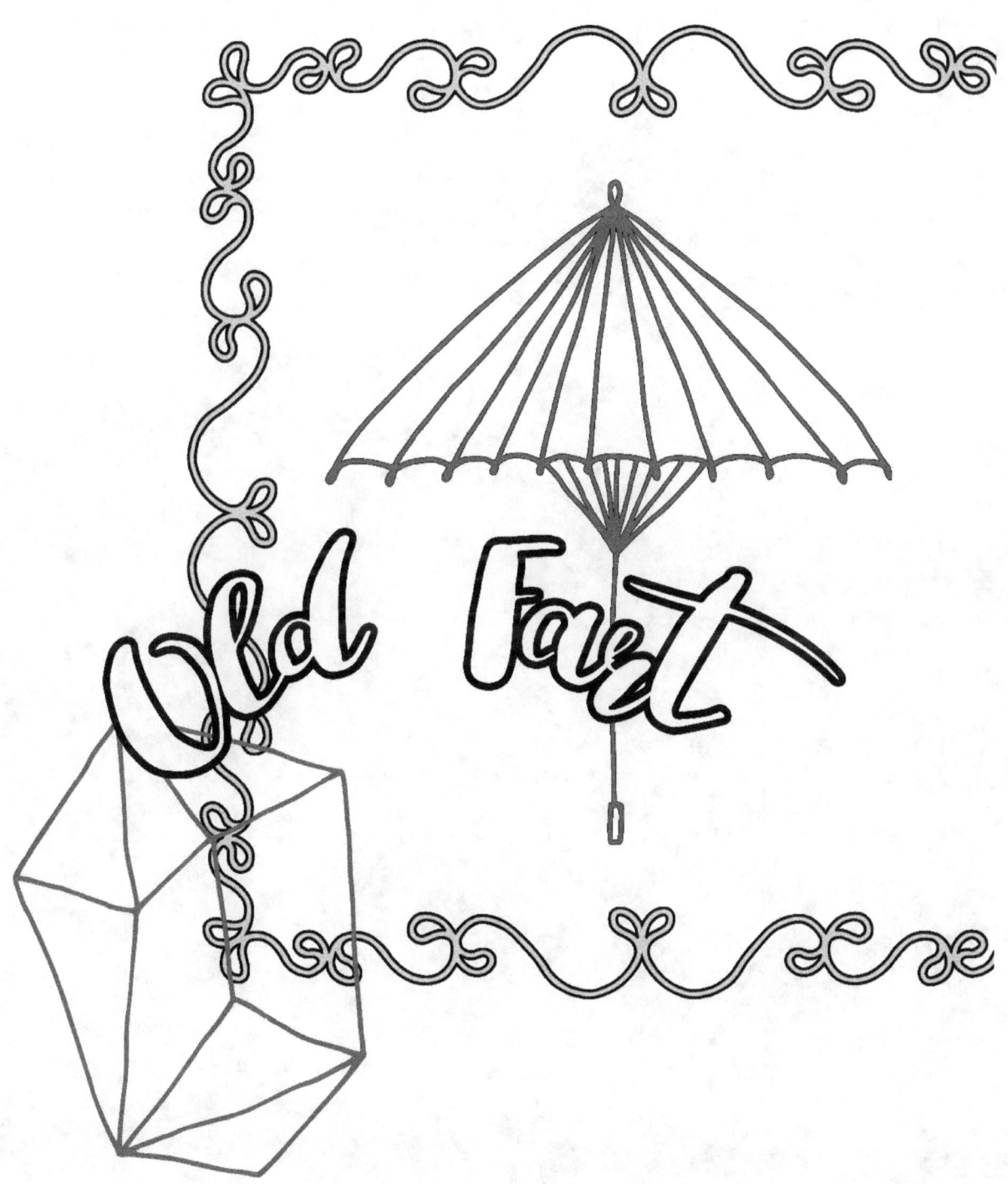

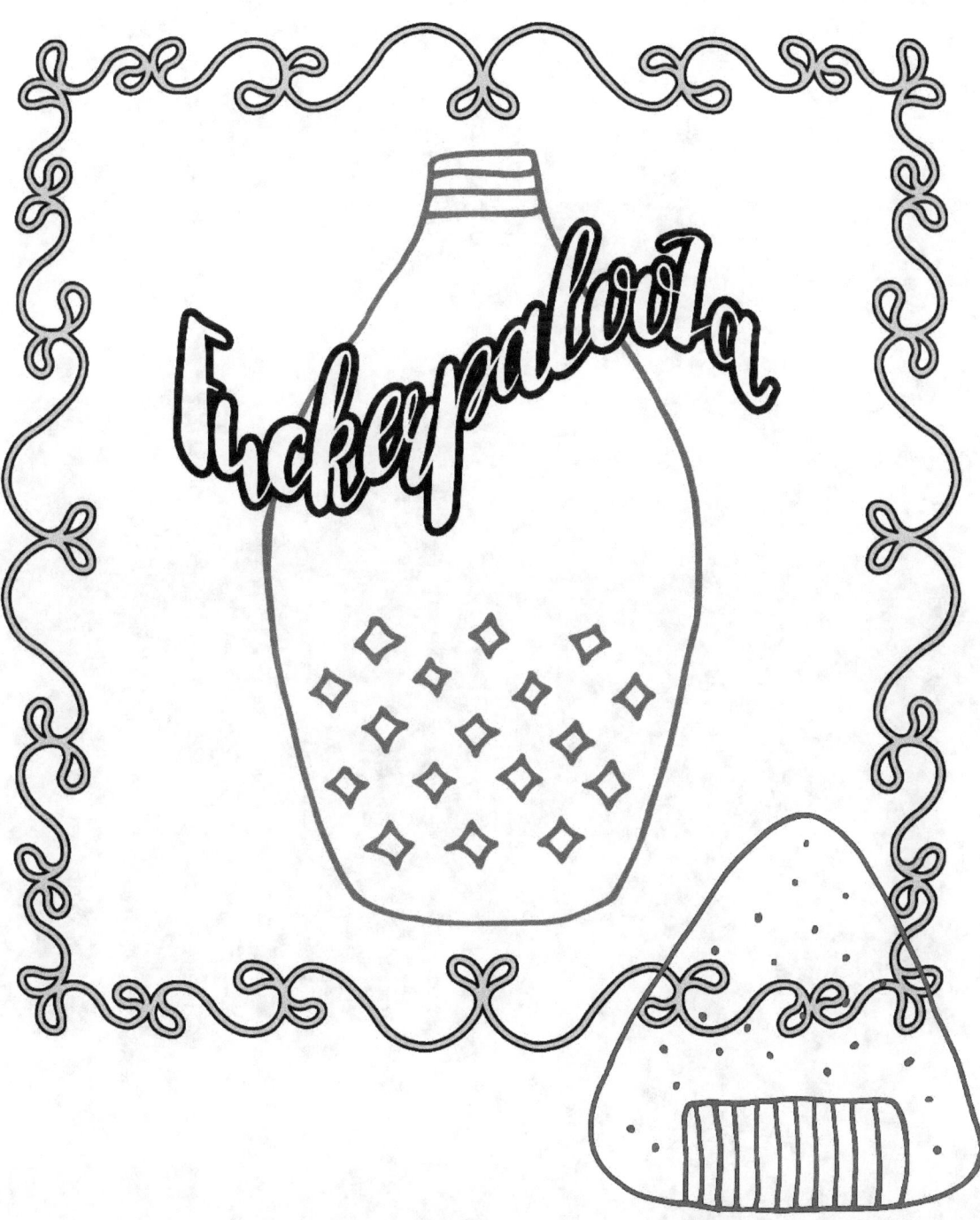

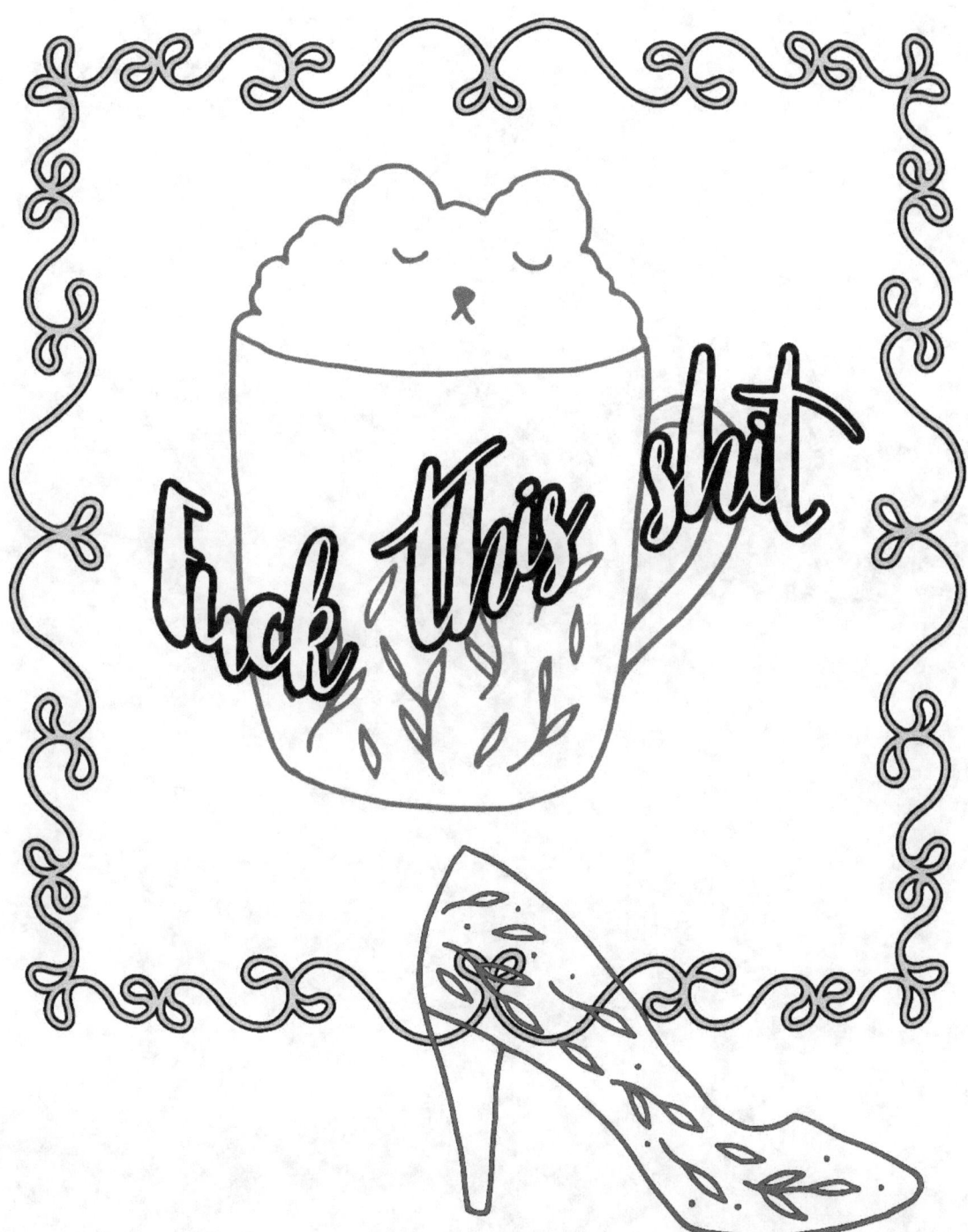

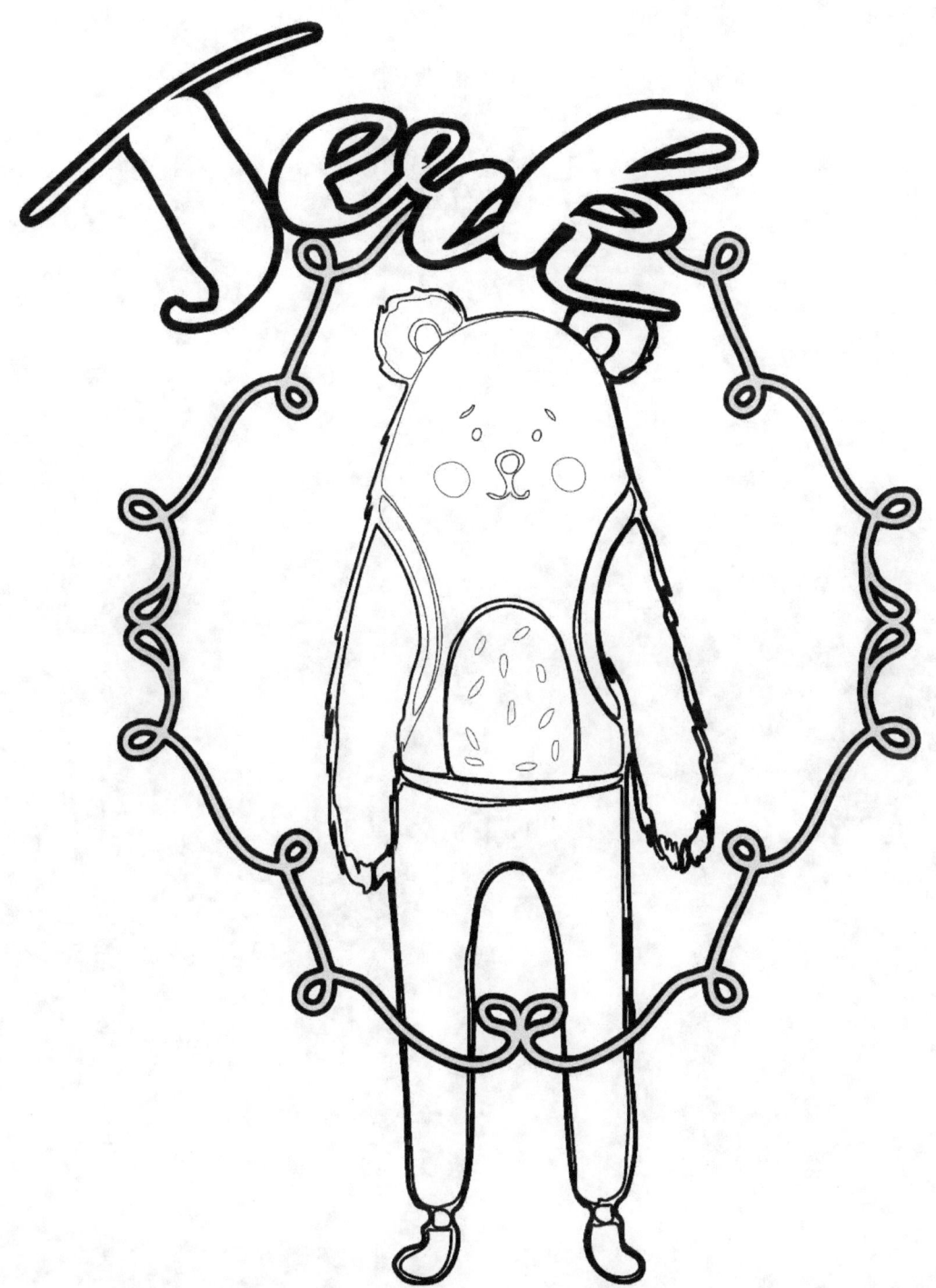

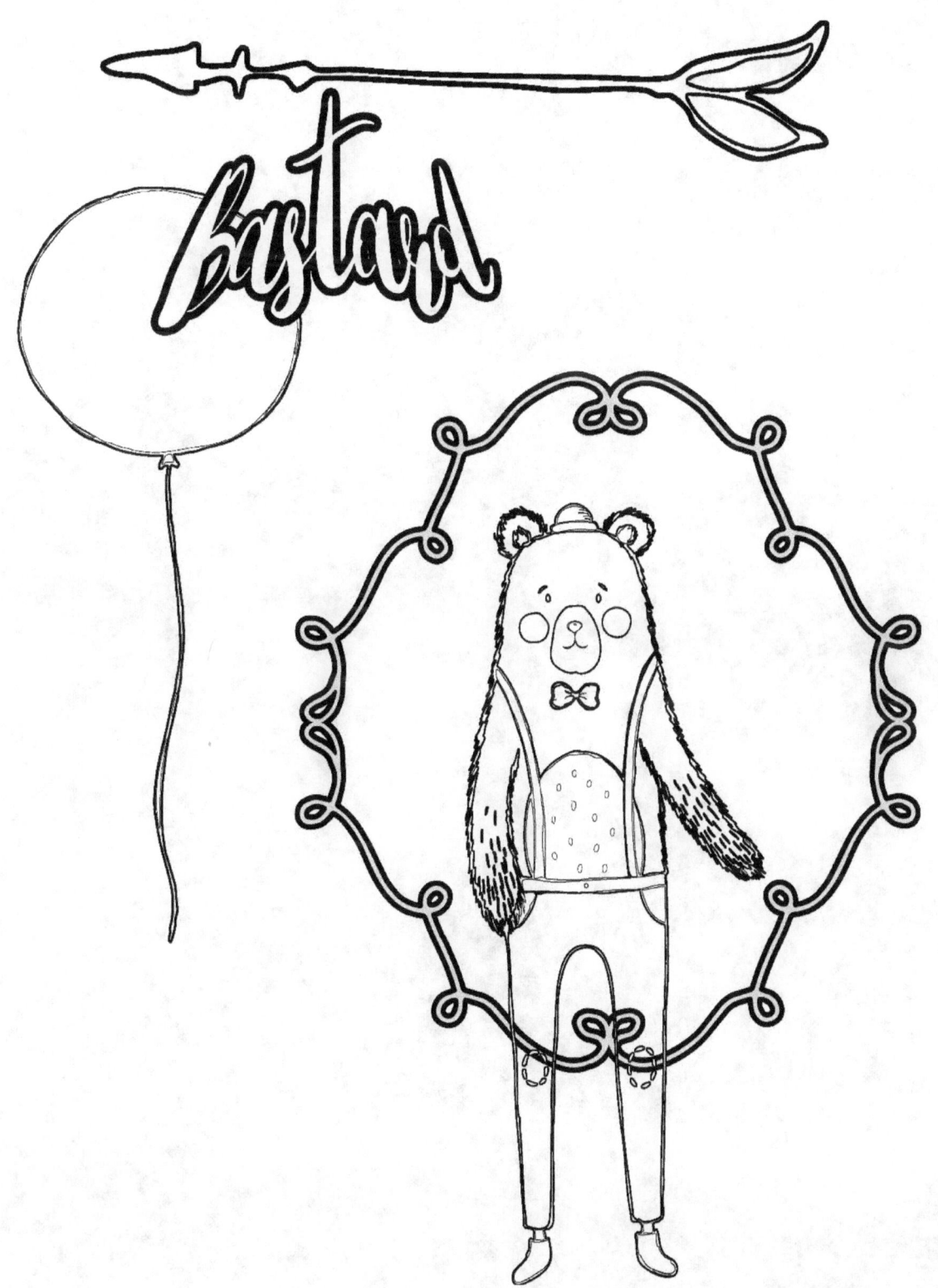

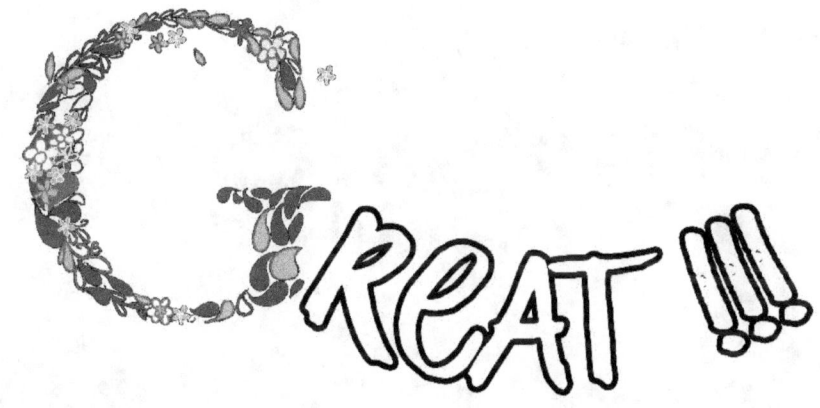

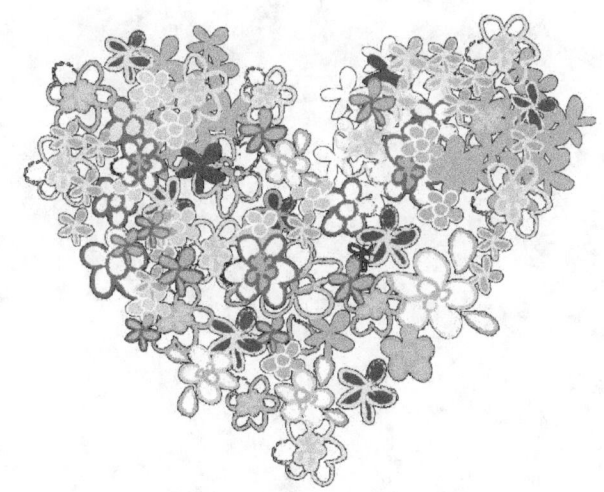

www.ingramcontent.com/pod-product-compliance
Lightning Source LLC
Chambersburg PA
CBHW081620220526
45468CB00010B/2959